# IT'S SCIENCE!

# Solid, liquid or gas?

## Sally Hewitt

# W
# FRANKLIN WATTS
### NEW YORK • LONDON • SYDNEY

First published in 1997 by Franklin Watts
96 Leonard Street, London EC2A 4RH

Franklin Watts Australia
14 Mars Road
Lane Cove
NSW 2066

Copyright © Franklin Watts 1997

Series editor: Rachel Cooke
Art director: Robert Walster
Designer: Mo Choy
Picture research: Susan Mennell
Photography: Ray Moller unless otherwise acknowledged
Consultant: Sally Nankivell-Aston

A CIP catalogue record for this book
is available from the British Library.

ISBN 0 7496 2842 1

Dewey Classification 530.4

Printed in Malaysia

Photographic acknowledgements:
Robert Harding pp. 10r, 19t, 26tl
John and Penny Hubley p. 17tr
Image Bank p. 6r, 13br, 24br
Magnum Photos p. 27tl (Steve McCurry)
Oxford Scientific Films p. 26br (Breck P. Kent/Earth Scenes)
Tony Stone pp. 26tr (Charles Krebs), 27tr (David Woodfall); Zefa p. 11bl
The publishers would also like to thank Tridias, 6 Bennett Street, Bath BA1 2QP 01225 314730 for their help with
some of the items featured on the title page and pp. 7, 14, 25 and 29.
Thank you, too, to our models: Claire Sutcliffe. Henry Cheese-Probert and Jordan Morris-Hudson

# Contents

# Useful materials

The things we use and see around us are made of all kinds of different **materials**.

Bricks, metal and glass are all materials that are good for building. They are all **solids**.

Can you spot bricks, metal and glass in this building? How has each one been used?

Cardboard, string, Plasticine and cotton wool are not good for making real buildings. But they are very useful materials. Why are they useful? The pictures will give you some ideas.

 **THINK ABOUT IT!**

What might happen if you built a real house out of cotton wool, string and cardboard?

 **TRY IT OUT!**

Look at some of the things around you, such as a carpet, a door or a spoon. Feel them as well. Do you know what materials they are made from?

# Pouring

Oil, washing-up liquid, honey and water are different kinds of **liquid**. Liquids can be poured.

**TRY IT OUT!**

Find 4 bowls and try pouring oil, washing-up liquid, honey and water into them. Which one pours very slowly? What happens to the liquid in the bowl?

Why do you think we usually keep liquids in containers? What other liquids can you think of?

Liquid does not have a **shape** of its own. Look what happens when the same amount of water is poured into these different shaped containers.

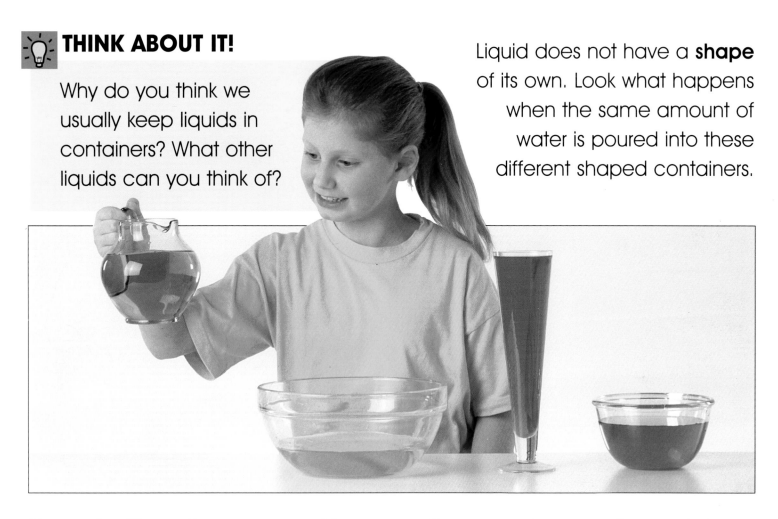

The water fills up the space and becomes the same shape as the container.

Salt and flour are not liquids but they can be poured because they are made up of thousands of tiny grains.

*Flour*

You can pour salt into a pile. Can you pour water into a pile too?

# Gas

Did you know that **air** is a kind of **gas**? We can't see it but it is all around us.

You breathe air in and out of your lungs.

 **TRY IT OUT!**

Blow into a balloon. You can see the air you breathe filling out the balloon. Let the air escape and feel it rushing out of the balloon.

This balloon is filled with a kind of gas called helium. Helium is lighter than air, so the balloon **floats** upwards.

Hot air is lighter than cold air so a hot air balloon floats upwards, too.

A car engine burns **fuel** and gives off a kind of gas called exhaust.

A burning fire gives off a kind of gas called smoke.

At first, you can see smoke and exhaust, then they mix into the air and you can't see them any more.

We burn natural gas for cooking and keeping warm.

11

# Water

Water is a very important liquid. We need water to drink to stay healthy and to wash in to keep clean.

Plants need water to grow.

**THINK ABOUT IT!**

Why do boats need water?
Why do firefighters need water?
What other ways do we use water?

Water is not always a liquid.
When it is cooled and **freezes,**
it becomes ice. Ice is a solid.

When water is heated up it becomes
steam. Steam is a gas.

 **LOOK AGAIN**

Find some solid materials on page 6.
Find some liquids on page 8.
Find some gases on pages 10 and 11.

An iceberg is a gigantic block of frozen water.
When the sun warms it, the ice **melts** back
into water again and mixes with the sea.

# Water test

Some things will float and some will **sink** when you put them in water.

The duck floats and so do all these other objects.

Marbles, a spoon and a pebble sink.

Look at the different objects on this page. Do you think they are heavy or light? Do you know what they are made of?

**TRY IT OUT!**

Collect some objects together. Guess whether the objects will float or sink. Put them in a bowl of water to see if you were right.

When you put some materials in water, they soak up the water and feel soggy.

Other materials don't soak up water at all. They are called **waterproof**.

### TRY IT OUT!

Find some brown paper, some plastic, a sponge and some wool. Feel them. Then guess what will happen when you put them in the water. Which ones will soak up water? Try it out to see if you were right.

15

# Melting

Butter, chocolate and a wax candle are all solid.

When they are heated, they melt and become liquid.

They become solid again when they cool down.

## TRY IT OUT!

Ask an adult to help you melt some chocolate in a bowl over a saucepan of simmering water. Pour the melted chocolate into pastry cutters. When the chocolate cools, it will set into new shapes.

Plastic melts and becomes soft and runny when it is heated.

Melted plastic can be poured into a **mould**. When it cools down, it sets into a the shape of the mould.

Look around you to find some things like these that are made of moulded plastic.

Metal melts when it is heated to a very high temperature. Molten metal was poured into a mould to make this toy truck.

# Changing shape

Clay is a kind of mud.
You can squash, press and roll
it into new shapes.

When clay is fired in a **kiln**, it dries out
and becomes hard. You can't
change the shape of a fired pot –
unless you smash it!

Pastry dough is soft and can be
made into new shapes.
When pastry is cooked, it hardens
and becomes good to eat!

## 👁 LOOK AGAIN

Look again at page 17.
What happens to metal and plastic when they are heated?

Thin sheets of metal can be cut, hammered and pressed into new shapes.

You can curl, twist and bend wire. It is good for making models because it will stay in its new shape.

### THINK ABOUT IT!

What else could you use wire for?

19

# Dissolving

If you look at salt and sugar through a magnifying glass, you will see hundreds of tiny **crystals**.

Salt and sugar crystals **dissolve** when they are mixed with water and make a **solution**.

 **TRY IT OUT!**

Mix a dessert-spoonful of sugar in half a glass of warm water. Keep stirring until the sugar disappears.

Dip your finger in the solution you have made and taste it. You can't see the sugar but you can taste that it is still there.

20

Look what happens when you mix cooking oil with water. It breaks up. But it will not dissolve however hard you stir.

**TRY IT OUT!**

Mix a spoonful each of instant coffee, tea leaves and jam in separate cups of warm water. Do any of them seem to 'disappear' like sugar? What happens to the colour of the water? Which one will not dissolve?

21

# Paper

Did you know that paper is made from tiny pieces of wood mixed with water to make wood **pulp**?

The pulp is squeezed out and rolled into sheets of paper.

 **TRY IT OUT!**

Collect different kinds of paper like these. Feel them. Try writing on them, tearing, folding and cutting them.
Which one is best for cutting?
Which ones tear easily?

Which paper on the opposite page would you use to write a letter?

Which paper would you use to wrap a present?

Which paper would be good for mopping up?

Which paper could you use to wrap sandwiches?

## 💡 THINK ABOUT IT!

Paper is used in hundreds of different ways.
How many ways of using paper can you think of?

23

# What material?

Do you know what this dining room chair, the baby's bowl and mug, the saucepan and the window panes are made of?

Can you think why they are made of each type of material?
Look at the opposite page to help you work out the answers.

Wood can be cut and carved.
It is strong but it burns easily.

Metal is strong and does not
burn easily.

Plastic is tough and light. It can be
moulded into different shapes.

You can see through glass
and it breaks easily.

 **THINK ABOUT IT!**

Glass would not be a good material for making a mug for a baby.
Why not? Could a saucepan be made of wood?

# Natural or made?

Some of the materials we use are **natural**.
They come from animals, plants and from the ground.

Wool comes from a sheep's soft coat.

Wood comes from trees, the biggest plants of all.

Marble is a kind of rock.

Some rocks have gold buried in them.

👁 **LOOK AGAIN**

Look again at page 18 to find another natural material.

Natural materials can be used to make different kinds of materials.

Oil from deep under the ground is used to make material called nylon.

Sand is one of the materials used to make glass.

 **LOOK AGAIN**

Look again at page 22 to find another **made** material.

27

# Useful words

**Air**  Air is a kind of gas. We can't see it but it is all around us. People, animals and plants all need air to live.

**Crystals**  Some solids are made up of flat-sided shapes called crystals. Tiny grains of sugar and salt are crystals.

**Dissolve**  When a solid mixes in with water and seems to disappear, we say it dissolves.

**Float**  Boats float on water. Balloons can float in air. They do not sink under the water or down to the ground.

**Freeze**  When water is cooled and turns into ice, we say it freezes.

**Fuel**  Fuel, such as oil, is something we burn to make energy.

**Gas**  The air around us is a kind of gas, so is steam from boiling water.  A gas does not have a shape of its own.

**Kiln**  A kiln is a type of oven where clay pots are dried out, or fired, at very high temperatures.

**Liquid**  Water, milk and oil are all kinds of liquid. Liquid can be poured and it does not have a shape of its own.

**Made**  Some materials we use, such as plastic and paper, are made by people. We call them made materials.

**Materials**  Wood, glass and paper are all different materials. Materials are what things are made of.

**Melt**  When a solid is heated and turns into a liquid, we say it melts.

**Mould**  A mould is a hollow shape which is used to give its shape to something, such as plastic.

**Natural**  A plant, an insect and a rock have not been made by people. They are all natural.

**Pulp**  Pulp is a slushy mixture of tiny pieces of wood and water used to make paper.

**Shape**  Every solid object has it own shape. A pencil is a long, thin shape and a ball is a round shape.

**Sink**  Some things, such as a rock or a coin, will not float on water. They sink down into it.

**Solid**  Solid things are neither liquid nor gas. They have shape of their own.

**Solution**  When some crystals, such as sugar and salt, are mixed with water, they dissolve and make a solution.

**Waterproof**  Some materials are waterproof. When they are put in water, they do not soak it up at all.

# Index

## About this book

Children are natural scientists. They learn by touching and feeling, noticing, asking questions and trying things out for themselves. The books in the *It's Science!* series are designed for the way children learn. Familiar objects are used as starting points for further learning. *Solid, liquid or gas?* starts with building bricks and explores materials.

Each double page spread introduces a new topic, such as liquids. Information is given, questions asked and activities suggested that encourage children to make discoveries and develop new ideas for themselves.
Look out for these panels throughout the book:

**TRY IT OUT!** indicates a simple activity, using safe, materials, that proves or explores a point.
**THINK ABOUT IT!** indicates a question inspired by the information on the page but which points the reader to areas not covered by the book.
**LOOK AGAIN** introduces a cross-referencing activity which links themes and facts through the book.

Encourage children not to take the familiar world for granted. Point things out, ask questions and enjoy making scientific discoveries together.